BACKYARD SAFARI

Blue Jays

Wil Mara

Cavendish
Square

New York

Published in 2015 by Cavendish Square Publishing, LLC
243 5th Avenue, Suite 136, New York, NY 10016

Copyright © 2015 by Cavendish Square Publishing, LLC

First Edition

Website: cavendishsq.com

This publication represents the opinions and views of the author based on his or her personal experience, knowledge, and research. The information in this book serves as a general guide only. The author and publisher have used their best efforts in preparing this book and disclaim liability rising directly or indirectly from the use and application of this book.

CPSIA Compliance Information: Batch #WS14CSQ

All websites were available and accurate when this book was sent to press.

Library of Congress Cataloging-in-Publication Data

Mara, Wil.
Blue jays / Wil Mara.
pages cm. — (Backyard safari)
Includes index.
ISBN 978-1-62712-834-6 (hardcover) ISBN 978-1-62712-835-3 (paperback) ISBN 978-1-62712-836-0 (ebook)
1. Blue jay—Juvenile literature. I. Title.

QL696.P2367M353 2014
598.8′64—dc23

2013047680

Editorial Director: Dean Miller
Editor: Andrew Coddington
Copy Editor: Cynthia Roby
Art Director: Jeffrey Talbot
Designer: Joseph Macri
Photo Researcher: J8 Media
Production Manager: Jennifer Ryder-Talbot
Production Editor: David McNamara

The photographs in this book are used by permission and through the courtesy of: Cover photo by Alina Morozova/Flickr/Getty Images; © Read, Marie/Animals Animals, 4; Michael G McKinne/Shutterstock.com, 5; Donald M. Jones/Minden Pictures/Getty Images, 6; Nancy Rose/Flickr Open/Getty Images, 8; © Read, Marie/Animals Animals, 9; © age fotostock/Alamy, 11; Stephen J. Krasemann/Photographer's Choice/Getty Images, 12; © Read, Marie/Animals Animals, 15; Fuse/Getty Images, 18; Tim Zurowski/All Canada Photos/Getty Images, 19; Paul Reeves Photography/Shutterstock.com, 21; imagebroker.net/SuperStock, 21; Animals Animals/SuperStock, 21; Catcher of Light, Inc./Shutterstock.com, 21; © Ardea/Zipp, Jim/Animals Animals, 22; Steve Cole/Vetta/Getty Images, 24; © Daybreak Imagery./Animals Animals, 26; Jessica Nelson/Flickr/Getty Images, 27.

Printed in the United States of America

Contents

Introduction

Have you ever watched a squirrel chasing another squirrel around a tree, or a group of deer leaping gracefully through a stretch of winter woods? If you have, then you know how wonderful it is to discover nature for yourself. Each book in the Backyard Safari series takes you step-by-step on an easy outdoor adventure, and then helps you identify the animals you've found. You'll also learn ways to attract, observe, and protect these valuable creatures. As you read, be on the lookout for the Safari Tips and Trek Talk facts sprinkled throughout the book. Ready? The fun starts just steps from your back door!

ONE
A Blue Jay's Life

A blue jay is considered a relatively medium-sized bird. The average length of an adult ranges from 9 to 12 inches (23 to 30 centimeters) and its **wingspan** measures about 15 to 16 inches (38 to 41 cm). A blue jay generally weighs between 2.5 and 3.75 ounces (70.8 and 106.3 grams). It is best known for its striking blue coloration, which is most visible along its back (down to the tip of its tail feathers) and the top of its head. The bird's chest and the underside of its tail can range in color from a medium gray to a vivid white. There are similar light markings around the eye and at the edges of some feathers. A blue jay also has a dark (usually black) U-shape pattern circling its neck and **crest**. Other dark marks occur in lines across some of its tail feathers. The bird's beak, legs, and claws are also dark. Overall, the blue jay is a very beautiful bird.

Blue jays get their name from the rich and beautiful coloration on many of their feathers.

One of the more interesting features of the blue jay is the small crown of feathers that form its crest. When the bird is calm and relaxed, the crest will rest flat on its head. When it's angry or alarmed, however, the crest will begin to rise to a height that indicates the bird's level of agitation. It is also interesting to note that male and female blue jays are basically identical, which makes it difficult to tell them apart in the wild. Males will grow a bit larger than females, but not much larger.

The feathers on top of a blue jay's head are called its "crest." When the crest is raised, it means the jay is alarmed or angered.

Trek Talk

Blue jays aren't really as blue as you think. Their "blueness" appears quite vivid because there are structures within their feathers that absorb other colors when hit by sunlight. This same light actually causes the blue coloring to appear more intense.

A beam of light contains many different colors. Certain surfaces, when the light hits them, will break up and absorb those colors, while others will reflect them. A blue jay's feathers are a perfect example of this type of surface. The reddish wavelengths in a light beam will be captured, while the blue wavelengths are scattered about. This makes the feathers' bluish coloring appear more vivid to the human eye. It's not the feathers that are so intensely blue, but the segment of a light beam being reflected back to your eye.

Where They Live

The blue jay is found mostly in the central and eastern regions of the United States. Populations also exist in southeastern and south-central Canada. Although many **species** of bird are migratory—meaning they move to warmer areas during the colder months—most blue jay populations remain in their **habitat** year round. In the most northern parts of their **range**, including the extreme northern United States and

Nuts, acorns, seeds, and berries make up the bulk of a blue jay's diet.

southern Canada, there are populations that will **migrate** south during the winter. The size of a migrating group can vary tremendously, from just a handful to many hundreds. Despite these numbers, most blue jays do not migrate. It is interesting to note that blue jay populations in certain areas have been known to migrate one year and stay put the next—a trend **ornithologists** cannot yet explain.

Blue jays are strong, intelligent birds that can survive in difficult surroundings. They can be found in all types of forested areas among any number of tree species. They do, however, have a fondness for oak trees. Blue jays are fairly comfortable around humans and can adapt to living in both suburban and more densely populated areas.

What They Do

The blue jay is a **diurnal** creature, meaning that it is most active during daylight hours. It is also among the most aggressive of all bird species. For example, it is quite **territorial** and will go to great lengths to protect its habitat range. It will attack any animal that it considers an invader, and not just other bird species. They are known to attack reptiles, such as snakes and lizards, as well as a variety of mammals including raccoons, squirrels, badgers, bats, cats, dogs, and even humans.

Blue jays become particularly alarmed when protecting their nests or young. They will fly wildly and let out a succession of shrill, or

Blue jays are not known for being particularly friendly! When they feel threatened, they will become quite aggressive, flapping their wings and making loud noises.

high-pitched, sounds as they use their beak and claws as weapons against invaders. Sometimes several blue jays will join together and descend upon an intruder. This group attack is called mobbing.

Blue jays also fight for feeding opportunities. They often do this by using their ability to mimic the sounds of other birds. Sometimes blue jays mimic hawks, a known **predator**, when approaching feeders. This sound tricks the birds that are feeding and causes them to scatter. The blue jays then take over the feeder.

The blue jay is considered an **omnivore**, meaning it eats both plant and animal matter. Although the bulk of its diet is made up of nuts, acorns, seeds, grains, and berries, it will on occasion feed on **invertebrates**, such as worms and insects. It is also known to eat small eggs and even the newborns of other bird species. A blue jay searches for food both on and off the ground. Its powerful beak is used to crack open shells while holding them between its claws. A blue jay is also happy to make a meal of whatever food items humans leave behind.

The Cycle of Life

Blue jays mate during the spring and early summer. Males and females stay together for a long time, often for life. Together they work to build a bowl-shaped nest using twigs, bark, and other plant matter gathered mostly by the male. They also use bits of human-made materials that help strengthen the nest's structure or soften its interior. The nest is built in any number of places, from dense shrubs to leafy trees, usually at a height of anywhere from 10 to 30 feet (3 to 9 meters). The average number of eggs in a **clutch** is four to five. The female will care for them while the male provides food for her. The eggs, which are bluish or light brown in color with brownish spots, will hatch in two to three weeks. Both male and female blue jays care for their newborns, or hatchlings. The young are ready for flight in about three weeks. They may fly with their parents for a short time before going out on their own. Young blue jays are highly susceptible to predators, but those that reach full adulthood in the wild usually live about six to eight years.

Mother blue jays often remain in the nest and care for the young, while the father will go out and collect food to bring back.

TWO

You Are the Explorer

Bird watching is one of the most relaxing and rewarding outdoor activities imaginable. There are many people of all ages and from all parts of the world who enjoy this pastime. Blue jays can be interesting study subjects because of their inherent beauty and active lifestyles. This means that there's plenty of activity to observe. Always remember that blue jays are highly aggressive, and sometimes even downright nasty. They won't hesitate to go after humans if they feel threatened enough. This is one bird that is best observed from a safe distance!

What Do I Wear?

* Clothes that aren't too bright or vivid in color—remember you don't want to draw unnecessary attention to yourself
* Clothes that are loose-fitting and comfortable
* Old clothes that can get dirty
* A jacket, gloves, hat, and other warm clothing if you are going out during cold weather
* Any type of shoes will do, but those with soft soles will be the quietest. Also, if you have to do a lot of walking, you'll want to be comfortable. In the winter, you might need boots.
* Bug spray, particularly if you're going into forested areas during the warmer months. Make sure you have a repellent for ticks, particularly if you live in the northeastern United States where they are common.

What Do I Take?

* Binoculars. A good pair of binoculars will be the most important piece of equipment you can bring along on your safari. Again, distance

is best when observing active blue jays. They are tolerant of, or willing to accept, human company—but only to a point.

* Folding chair or blanket
* Notebook
* Pen or pencil
* Digital camera, particularly one that can retain good focus while zooming
* Cellphone
* A snack for yourself

Where Do I Go?

You should be able to find a few blue jays within a reasonable distance of your home. They are the most active during the day, as they forage for food both on and off the ground. They like to harass anyone they view as a threat, but if you're willing to remain at a safe distance, you should be able to observe them without any problems.

* Wooded areas. Blue jays like forested areas as much as any other wild animal. They don't require the same degree of privacy and cover as some other birds except when caring for their young. During those times their nests can be almost impossible to find. They build their nests high off the ground,

so your binoculars will come in handy. You don't have to be particularly concerned with the type of woodland you explore, as blue jays can make their homes in all types of forests. They are, however, more abundant near forest edges than in heavily wooded areas.

❋ Thick shrubs and other overgrowth. During breeding season—most of the spring and into part of the summer—blue jays will build their nests in places where their young will be most protected. This is usually in shrubs and hedges, or any other area that has thick overgrowth. If you do find a blue jay nest, feel free to observe it—but don't get too close.

❋ Your backyard. Blue jays seem comfortable sharing their world with humans as long as they are left alone. If your property has a fair number of trees, you should be able to spot a blue jay's nest without too much trouble. Even beyond the breeding season, blue jays still spend much of their time searching for food. That makes it possible to observe the birds right outside your bedroom window.

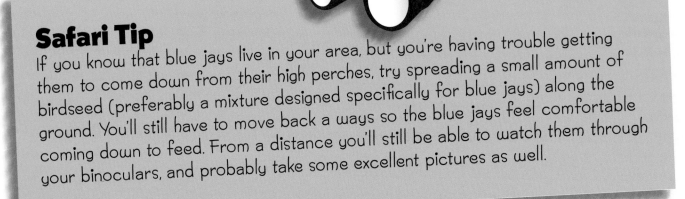

Safari Tip

If you know that blue jays live in your area, but you're having trouble getting them to come down from their high perches, try spreading a small amount of birdseed (preferably a mixture designed specifically for blue jays) along the ground. You'll still have to move back a ways so the blue jays feel comfortable coming down to feed. From a distance you'll still be able to watch them through your binoculars, and probably take some excellent pictures as well.

It can be dangerous for you to walk around alone, so you should always be with an adult that you trust when you go on a blue jay safari. You should also make sure you have permission if your safari takes you to someone else's property. Wooded areas, for example, are a great place to find blue jays—but not if they are private property and you aren't allowed to be there. You can get into serious trouble for trespassing.

What Do I Do?

❊ Go out during the day. Remember that blue jays are diurnal creatures, which means they rest during the night. You should look for them when they will be fully rested and ready for their daily activities, and this means very early in the morning.

You can also go out just before sunset. That is when the blue jays feel a bit safer searching for food as their presence is less obvious to predators.

❋ Listen. Blue jays are quite vocal—and this will help you on your safari. You can find sound samples of their calls online. Different bird species make distinct sounds, which help expert bird watchers identify a bird. You can also learn this skill. Once you've become familiar with that unique blue jay sound, you'll be amazed how easily you can locate one in the wild. Many bird-watchers locate specimens by hearing them before seeing them.

❋ Be patient. This might be the most important safari tip of all. You probably won't spot a blue jay within the first ten minutes of your safari. That's normal. They are always targets for predators, so blue jays are experts at sensing danger. They'll know you're coming toward them long before you know *they're* there.

❋ Don't make distracting noises or movements. Blue jays easily become nervous when they spot "invaders." Once you've located a blue jay, find a safe observation spot and remain there. If you're quiet and still, the bird will feel more comfortable and continue its business. That's the point of your safari, after all.

* Have your camera ready at all times. Blue jay safaris are great opportunities to capture a few great pictures of these beautiful birds. Always keep your camera on. There may not be time to turn it on when a blue jay flies or lands near you Also, avoid using a flash. The bright light could startle the blue jay.

* Make notes. Write down anything that you feel is important while observing the blue jays. Where were you when you saw them? What were they doing? What time of day was it? After you gather enough information, you'll begin to recognize patterns that'll help you with future safaris.

* Download any pictures you took when you return home. Show them to your friends and family. You could also write a formal journal using both your pictures and your notes. Keep an ongoing record of your blue jay safaris from year to year.

THREE

A Guide To Blue Jays

There is only one species of blue jay, *Cyanocitta cristata*, and four **subspecies**: northern blue jay, coastal blue jay, interior blue jay, and Florida blue jay. These subspecies are considered fairly "weak" because there is little difference between them. However, there is another blue jay known as Steller's Jay (*Cyanocitta stelleri*), which is also quite beautiful. This bird can be found in the evergreen forests of western North America, as well as campgrounds, picnic areas,

The blue jay shares its genus, *Cyanocitta*, with just one other species — *Cyanocitta stelleri*, the Stellar's jay, shown here.

parks, and backyards. Let's examine some important points that should help successfully identify the blue jay you encounter.

Referring back to the notes you made while you were on your safari, consider the following questions:

* Is the blue jay's blue coloration bright and vivid, or is it somewhat dull?
* Is the coloration a medium shade of blue, or is it fairly dark?
* Is the bird smaller in size even though it is an adult?
* Was the chest coloration lighter (whitish or a light to moderate yellow) or darker (fair to medium gray)?
* Were there many black markings along the blue feathers?
* Is the bird half black or dark gray on top and half blue below?
* Is its crest pure black and very pronounced?
* Are there a few small white markings on the crest?

After you've made your notes, go to the next page and see if any of the blue jays in the photos match the **characteristics** of the blue jays you saw. Your location (town, state, country) and the time of year your observations were made are also important to keep in mind. This is especially true if you live in the western half of the United States or in Central America, where the blue jay and the Steller's Jay may breed together. Try doing a little research on the Internet, too. The books and websites provided for you in this book's "Find Out More" section are great places to start.

Northern blue jay

Coastal blue jay

Interior blue jay

Florida blue jay

FOUR
Try This!
Projects You Can Do

Blue jays are not suitable for house pets, but you can always go into the wild and visit them. You can also further your interest in blue jays through working on several hands-on projects when you're not busy on one of your safaris. Here are a few fun and easy projects that you can integrate into your blue jay activities.

Home Building

One fun project you can do is building a blue jay birdhouse to keep in your backyard. The most important detail to remember is that blue jays only need a very simple house. The house you build only needs a base, a roof, and walls on only two opposite sides. (Make sure to leave the front and back wide open so the blue jays can fly in and out.)

What Do I Need?

* ❇ Wood boards
* ❇ A hammer and nails
* ❇ Paint (optional)
* ❇ Tree or wooden pole
* ❇ Ladder

What Do I Do?

* ❇ After you have gathered your materials, begin constructing the birdhouse. You should always have an adult help you with such a project, of course, since it may require the use of power tools.

* ❇ The roof and base do not need to be any larger than 8 inches (20 cm) square. The walls should be roughly the same in height, and with a depth of no more than 10 inches (25 cm).

❊ You can either leave your house unpainted or add colorful designs. The blue jays won't mind. It's important to remember that birds could have a reaction to paints that are oil-based, though, so make sure to only use water-based paints.

❊ When your house is finished and the paint has dried, pick a quiet area in your backyard to place your birdhouse. Have an adult help you hang the birdhouse off the side of a tree or place it on top of a pole. The higher you can place your birdhouse, the better.

Building a birdhouse can be very rewarding, but you should not try it without the assistance of an adult.

Feeding Time

Blue jays are opportunistic at mealtime and are perfectly happy taking food from birdfeeders. You could build one, but they're so inexpensive that it's probably not worth the trouble. If you go to your local home-improvement center or department store you'll probably find a wide variety of them.

What Do I Need?

* Birdfeeder
* Birdseed
* A tree

What Do I Do?

* Hang the feeder wherever you'd like. Blue jays, as you now know, search for food both on the ground and in the air. Just make sure the feeder isn't too close to your house, as they may be disturbed by the human activity.
* Once you have hung your birdfeeder, fill it with food blue jays will eat. There are a variety of birdseeds and other bird treats you can buy, including some blends that are specially made for blue jays.

A birdfeeder will attract blue jays and other birds and can brighten a backyard — even in winter.

✳ Once your local blue jays discover the feeder, they'll be visiting quite often (as will other birds and even a few squirrels). That means you'll have to refill it frequently. Make sure to keep your feeder full of food to keep your blue jay neighbors stopping by.

Talk and More Talk

Blue jays are very vocal birds. They use their calls to communicate with one another. You can learn these calls, too! With a little practice, you can converse with the blue jays you find on your safari.

What Do I Need?

* ❋ Your hands and voice
* ❋ A bush or tree to hide behind

What Do I Do?

* ❋ The first step in this activity is to learn as many blue jay sounds as possible. You can find hundreds of blue jay sound files on the Internet.
* ❋ Practice making these calls until you feel that yours are similar to the ones made by real blue jays. They don't have to be perfect, but try to get as close as possible.

Learning to imitate bird sounds takes practice, but it'll be worth it when you're on safari.

※ When you spot a blue jay on one of your safaris, listen to the sounds it's making, then try to make the same sound on your own. The real excitement will come when you draw the bird's attention to you. You may get it to call back, or even fly closer to you. If it does, you have a perfect opportunity to take more great photos and make some terrific notes.

First Aid

There is always a chance that you could come across a blue jay that is sick or wounded during one of your safaris. A hurt blue jay would be moving slowly, unable to fly, or lying on the ground. You may be tempted to get closer to the bird to try and help. Don't! First, you could frighten the bird very badly. The bird may also be carrying a disease that can be very harmful. Again, blue jays aren't big fans of human contact, so an injured blue jay could still have enough strength to harm you. If you have an adult with you (which you should), ask that person to call your local animal control organization (most towns have them), zoo, or police department. If you see a blue jay that is suffering, be smart and let someone else take care of the situation. Don't try to handle it on your own.

Glossary

characteristic a specific trait or quality that an animal has, such as tan fur or brown eyes

clutch a nest of eggs

diurnal active during the day

habitat the exact type of place in which an animal lives

invertebrate an animal that does not have a backbone

migrate to move from one geographical location to another; many species of bird will move from one area to another at different times of the year

omnivore an animal that eats both plant and animal matter

ornithologist a zoologist who studies birds

predator an animal that hunts other animals for food

range the general area in which an animal lives

species one type of animal or plant within a larger category

subspecies an animal with a slight variation that separates it from others in its species, but not so much that it could be its own species

territorial a word that describes an animal that is protective of the area in which it lives

wingspan the length of a bird's wings from tip to tip when fully extended

Find Out More

Books

Cate, Annette LeBlanc. *Look Up! Bird-Watching in Your Own Backyard.* Somerville, MA: Candlewick Press, 2013.

Porter, Adele. *Wild About Northeastern Birds: A Youth's Guide.* Cambridge, MN: Adventure Publications, 2010.

Truit, Trudi Strain. *Birds.* New York: Cavendish Square, 2011.

Websites

Blue Jay / National Geographic

animals.nationalgeographic.com/animals/birds/blue-jay

Basic information about the blue jay can be found here along with some beautiful illustrations, a habitat range map, and bird audio files.

BioKids—Blue Jay

www.biokids.umich.edu/critters/Cyanocitta_cristata

Here you will find basic facts about various birds and some great photos of blue jays. There are links to other useful websites as well as useful reference materials.

Blue Jay / Cornell Lab of Ornithology ('All About Birds')

www.allaboutbirds.org/guide/blue_jay/sounds

This website provides excellent overall information about birds and a terrific selection of easy-to-play blue jay sound files.

Index

Page numbers in **boldface** are illustrations.

About the Author

WIL MARA is the award-winning author of more than 150 books. He began his writing career with several titles about herpetology—the study of reptiles and amphibians. Since then he has branched out into other subject areas and continues to write educational books for children. To find out more about Mara's work, you can visit his website at www.wilmara.com.